RESIST!
IN DEFENCE OF COMMUNISM

GUSTAAF PEEK

TRANSLATION BY / *VERTALING DOOR*
BRENDAN MONAGHAN

Resist! In Defence of Communism
by Gustaaf Peek

Translated from the Dutch
by Brendan Monaghan

First published in English
*by Strangers Press, Norwich, 2020
(part of UEA Publishing Project)*

Distributed
by NBN International

Printed
by Swallowtail Print, Norwich

All rights reserved
© 2017 by Gustaaf Peek,
published by Em. Querido's Uitgeverij
Translation
© Brendan Monaghan, 2020,
mentored by David Colmer

Editorial team
*Nathan Hamilton, David Colmer,
Michele Hutchison, Bas Pauw and Victor Schiferli*

Editorial assistance
by Senica Maltese, Brad Bigelow and Magdalena Steinhauser

Cover design and typesetting
by Office of Craig

The rights of Gustaaf Peek to be identified as the author and Brendan Monaghan to be identified as the translator of this work have been asserted in accordance with the Copyright, Designs and Patents Act, 1988. This booklet is sold subject to the condition that it shall not, by way of trade or otherwise, be lent, resold, hired out, stored in a retrieval system, or otherwise circulated without the publisher's prior consent in any form of binding or cover other than that in which it is published and without a similar condition including this condition being imposed on the subsequent purchaser.

ISBN-13: 978-1911343318

Resist!
In Defence of Communism

'In place of the old bourgeois society, with its classes and class antagonisms, we shall have an association, in which the free development of each is the condition for the free development of all.'

The Communist Manifesto by Karl Marx and Friedrich Engels

It's not too late. It is not too late.

Humanity starts again with every birth. We are born with our ancestors' biological inheritance, not knowledge of their experiences, mistakes or attainments. Every child has to learn how to live, how to be their own person amongst other people. Every generation encounters a world shaped by predecessors who tried to pass on their ideas of life and society. It's a reality no one can avoid, a crippling game of catch-up we can never finish. Time seems too short to correct old blunders, too complex to fix valuable insights in place and save the future from being tarnished by stubborn flaws.

The most blatant expression of human history is technology: how our clothes are sewn, how the fabric is manufactured; how we cultivate our fields, feed and slaughter our cattle, the routes by land and sea all this food travels to finally reach us; sewerage, combustion engines, the electricity that brings all our indispensable gadgets to life; wheelchairs, glasses, penicillin.

Although technology influences our lives down to the second and into our molecules, it's ideas that determine where we're going and control how we see ourselves and our environment. It's ideas that drive our thoughts and actions: how we see our role in our family or society; whether we believe in higher powers or hierarchies; what we deem valuable and important, and what not; what hardships we expect to endure; acceptable ways of expressing our talents and dreams.

Every idea originated at a specific moment in history. The moment demanded it: there was upheaval or chaos, a crisis to resolve or a vacuum to fill. Every idea starts as a promise. A vow to change something or make it permanent, to seize the unpredictable and uncertain present and turn it into a future, a more easily imaginable tomorrow. But the reality of a certain period is not the same as the reality people can neither escape nor ignore later. Circumstances change, as do insights. Ideas can change from friends to foes.

We are children of the Cold War. The post-war world seemed split in two. Both sides claimed to be the hero and saviour of history. In the Western version of the story, the United States had ineluctable right on its side; it was only a matter of time before the Soviet Union would realise that capitalism would decide the future. With its long queues for stale bread and the last toilet rolls, its unfashionable look and lack of freedom, the Soviet Union didn't stand a chance. We felt strengthened by our fully stocked shops, truthful newspapers and light-hearted television programmes, our free access to pop music.

Good versus evil. And behind this doctrinal struggle, both creeds' tanks roared. Wars raged in distant countries; enormous numbers of people were killed in a chilling test of strength. Even today, nuclear weapons wait patiently to settle any overly threatening discussion. Dictatorship or democracy, over the decades the political camps remained equally convinced that the other was their mortal enemy. Fearing for their lives, citizens on both sides could only look on.

Then, in November 1989, elated people swung pickaxes at the breached Berlin Wall, embraced each other, sang, celebrated their newfound freedom. We still feel the joy, so profoundly did we experience our connection with those who'd had to do without so much for so many years. Finally, we had all reached the same realisation: freedom cannot be restricted, no future without emancipation. Finally, winter had come to an end. From now on it would be glorious summer for everyone.

The freedom we knew is the freedom we have passed on. History had proved us right; why wait to see what reborn peoples or countries might come up with? Why keep questioning what had led to this glorious moment? Countries with newly open borders became markets and competitors; their citizens, customers and appealingly cheap migrant workers. We looked on with satisfaction as they made more and more money in their struggle to be like us.

Why? When did we start associating our joy at their liberation with a dominant theory of economics? Do we believe people smashed the Wall with pickaxes to let in capitalism? Were they dancing at the prospect of finally being able to compulsively accumulate? Were the choruses of their tearful songs about the opportunity to compete each other into the ground; did they embrace because of long-cherished dreams of overproduction and an abundance of consumer items?

For a while we let them have their naive dreams of freedom, but soon drove them towards our own realism. To our own myths that people with less money are lesser and deserve meagre, constrained lives. Our belief that the wealthy have earned and deserve their piles of gold, their freedom. Things just aren't fairly divided in this world. We're living in the end time and experiencing the zenith of human economic ingenuity. Class differences are natural and inevitable.

Why have we come to so regard power imbalances as logical and fair?

Whilst capitalism has clear historical origins, it has little regard for history and none at all for its lessons. There is only a present of destructive competition, disruptive takeovers and intimidating expropriation, and a future of infinite, irrational greed. As revolutionary as capitalism may appear, its dynamic is bitterly predictable. For every incredible success, there are countless victims. For every short and hierarchically rewarding boom, a protracted collective crisis. For every growth market, a scarred environment.

And capitalism feels constantly threatened, judging from the astronomical marketing budgets to convince us of its usefulness and beneficence; the staggering contributions to political campaigns and funding of lobbyists to keep leaders on the straight and narrow; and the use of political authority in the form of armies and economic sanctions to suppress ideologically threatening movements all over the world.

Autumn 2008. After many warning signs, the pioneers and quartermasters of the great historical truth, the banks, were hoisted en masse by their own petards. Economies proved to be as unreal as the banks' pyramid schemes, and a global financial crisis ensued. But where for years governments had used a litany of strict regulations to systematically cut back on the wellbeing of the societies in their care, vast funds were immediately available for the extremely costly rehabilitation of those who caused this economic collapse. The victims had to pay, suffer, and be made to believe they were the culprits.

Everyone fears an overwhelming force; nobody can choose freely in an emergency. There were no acute fires, no imminent floods, no hostile armies massing at the border. But still we saw our governments constantly take the side of the markets. So we backed the perpetrators in the voting booth. As cowed and timorous as in the Cold War, we surrendered to this stifling view of society, this irrational version of humanity.

We've often seen how temporary even firm convictions can be. Child labour, bloodletting, slavery. Burning people at the stake, denying women all rights, sparing the rod and spoiling the child. Colonialism, feudalism, a monarch's absolutist whims. A twelfth child on the priest's orders, arbitrary justice, an earth that can infinitely absorb every human encroachment. Man in God's image.

So many previous generations were so sure of their beliefs and ways of life.

We're not living at the end of history, or the dénouement of an inevitable development. Every era fades into the next. It is revealing how much history fluctuates. In the natural sciences there are real impossibilities, but the 'politically impossible' has been proven again and again to be nothing but a way station. After societies have shaken off the last of their capitalist ballast, we will look back in bewilderment: How was it ever possible for people to do that to each other?

Increasing autonomy and reducing fear. A realisation of the historical basis and effects of exploitation. Outlawing the forces and powers that propagate and sustain this exploitation. Developing political consciousness as a necessary prerequisite for social change. A truly egalitarian society with political organisations to match. The insight that solidarity guarantees unconditional political freedom, so democracy can fulfil its promise of representation and accountability. A world of equal opportunities, not unequal outcomes. The fair distribution of knowledge, power and income. All these elements are the essence of communism.

Nobody can predict the future; wise are they who promise nothing impossible to the present but see the future as a concrete process of endeavour and adaptation, inevitable failure and never-ending improvement. Wise are we when we refuse to empower frauds who — for short-term, personal interests — constrict our future and all its possibilities, trying to ensnare us in false predictions to suppress us even more forcefully in the present.

Humanity starts again with every birth. Burdening generations with an end time is a deliberate act of repression, yet another attempt to alienate us from ourselves and our human motivations for living. We have been chosen, but not to provide the one per cent with a structure to exploit us. We have been chosen because of the promise inherent in all our births — the freedom to live with dignity and love, to give meaning to our limited time on earth and safeguard the future for our loved ones.

I

Capital is a common effort. Before capital is amassed by accumulating proceeds of some kind or other, innumerable visible and invisible hands have been at work. Before any of us sit down at a desk, or start a workday in a warehouse or on a wharf; before any of us move goods or carry plates and glasses out to customers; before any of us repair, check or harvest anything, we crisscross our surroundings, having left our homes — the homes where we had breakfast in rooms we've decorated, on our own or with others, living with us, maybe loving us or supporting us in some other way; perhaps we're raising children or have some other intimate relationship, we've almost certainly taken someone or something into our heart, at first sight or after a longer exploration, one of the many defining moments of a human life, the moment of arriving somewhere, with someone or on your own, in any case having grown, after years of school, of falling down and getting up again, years of reading and mental arithmetic and all those first experiences in playgrounds and on playing fields, all that knowledge to help us understand nature and culture, whilst constantly listening to stories and making up new ones, years of sport perhaps, after moments of hesitant or lively dancing, years of meals and favourite dishes, all the conversations, all the birthday parties — friends and strangers around the table — all that time with loved ones, all the heads bowed at funerals, rising countless mornings after sleeping and dreaming, years of moving and travelling both near and far, years of caring for ourselves and others, who have been changed by our presence, unexpectedly influencing us in return, the way family, teachers, doctors, friends and guardians have helped us develop from a very young age, so many people who have contributed to our present — so many people whose future we devote our energy to through thick and thin — before any of us even *think* of work, we have already been shaped by the most crucial parts of human society.

Then we bring all this to work, to our jobs, all these experiences, which the big bosses don't have a clue about and haven't contributed to. Yet all these people and circumstances, all these unseen investments in their workers will certainly contribute to *them*. And for this our bosses pay us just enough to get by so we can work for them again the next day. What's happened?

Capital is a common effort pocketed by a single group. All that time, effort and energy to raise people, for us to simply exist, and we don't get anything of comparable value in return. Not only that, the added value of our existence and work is destined for our bosses and no one else. It's as if we've had to surrender our history so they can reinvest it in the conditions that generate their profit. The dividend of our lives goes to the one per cent. Our bosses profit financially from our lives more than we do.

Is that right? Is it fair?

Yet the problem is bigger. It's not just about money.

Capital cannot stand still, cannot be contented with what it has. The pursuit of maximised profit is never ending; once a production or profit target has been met, the end point becomes the starting point. Capital must grow and can only do so by breaking through limits. This restlessness and lack of inhibition have caused substantial and far-reaching technological progress and unprecedented private wealth. But the limits of tradition and technology are not the only things the pursuit of capital shatters. In its cravings for profit, capitalism lacks all moral or rational underpinning; it has no moderation, no human restraint. No sense of responsibility for clean drinking water, the ability to heal people, dress them warmly, house them properly. It will impatiently utilise anything no matter how harmful, heedlessly draining natural and human resources, and then sweeping on to new places and labour markets to bleed dry. And so on, and so forth.

For capitalism, exploitation is not to be regretted, but is a necessity. As an economic system it is literally exhausting, always yearning for more. Maintaining and intensifying our drudgery, our anxious attempts to make ends meet, is entirely intentional.

Who can still believe that capitalism will achieve its golden mean of supply and demand and that this might bring about a utopian balance? Who believes that a utopia of this sort might find natural economic solutions for all its failings? Who would bet their lives on capitalism?

As much as markets would have us believe they only produce what's needed, the unambiguous pursuit of profit really entails a simple dynamic: only what is most profitable is produced. And production driven solely by profit endangers humans. From the birth of capitalism some five centuries ago, there has been a gulf between capitalism's material potential and the dissemination of its proceeds to most people on earth. People still suffer from starvation, despite enough food for everyone. For the outrageous and neurotic fortunes of a few individuals, we breathe polluted air, drink water contaminated by plastic, till contaminated soil, and encounter the increasingly destructive effects of a warming earth. Our privacy is for sale, as is our health. Talent is left idle or used improperly for staggering sums. Capital could permanently fulfil the most important human needs but is simply unable to transcend its own principles. Even when companies invest in useful and valuable things like housing, news-gathering, pensions or environmentally friendly technology, these inveterate repeat offenders will over time still favour their own interests (in the form of overproduction, cost savings and price increases) over those of the common people.

We should have known better. In the sixteenth century, economic relations in the English countryside changed. For the time, English society had an extraordinarily strong central government, limiting landlords' opportunities to exploit their farmers. Fewer and fewer farmers owned land, and more and more landlords let their fields. They realised that leasing land to the most productive tenants increased their earnings. Tenants competed with each other, specialised, and tried new techniques to increase yields. A market came into being. Tenants no longer had secure tenancy. It was no longer about crops or livelihoods, but the profits their work could generate. All this upheaval and struggle gave landlords the greatest possible return, further increased by the privatisation of public land. Productivity took off; never before had so much been extracted from farmland. But the new profit maximisation also meant that fields and livestock had never been so prone to misuse, disruption and depletion. Many succumbed to the competition, creating a modern mass of paupers — the ideal ingredient for further developing capitalist principles in the cities.

A revolutionary experiment had been conducted on a basic human need: food. Food had been reduced to a commodity; never before had people eaten so little from their own land. This transformation is revealing. Capitalism seized hold of the human stomach early, making itself indispensable and necessary, impossible to reject without starving. From that point on, survival would be subject to the oppressive laws of the market.

Winners and losers. Both convinced of the fairness of their fates. How magical, how comforting. Winners must be careful not to lose their footing on the slippery slope, keeping them ambitious and wily; whilst there's always a chance the losers might one day summon the courage and zeal to become winners. There's a balance; everything might turn out all right.

How much violence does this do to reality? How deeply must we be sleeping to accept such an unjust dream?

Governments save banks and claim the balance from their citizens. How can we *not* speak of perpetrators and victims?

A sudden outbreak of incredible generosity and social consensus created a united political front — something which for decades had apparently proved impossible for expanding health care or improving education, or for food safety, accessible and reliable public transport, introducing a basic income or making a permanent switch to sustainable energy. When the banks were threatened with collapse, the customary arguments justifying budget discipline proved to be no more than myths for disciplining society, a means of promoting inequality and reinstating old power.

Nobody can vote for markets. Governments have outsourced so many social values and so much of our public property that votes in elections count less than a nod from private interests. No one can govern what they don't own. Once the family silver has been sold, it's gone for good. Parliament must seek the market's approval before contributing towards society in areas such as energy, defence, healthcare, childcare or telecommunications. Consent is only granted in exchange for pay-offs, in the form of money, *our* money, or political undertakings. Capital tries to draw every social achievement into its domain of the bottom line. Government may want to forbid something, but property comes with far-reaching rights.

Free trade. The free market. The freedom to enter into contracts with each other. Free will. How much freedom is possible when democratic authority is waning, when ever-greater imbalances in power determine relations?

Capitalism has its contradictions and secrets; most are very public by now. Markets grumble about government interference, about meddling and irksome red tape resulting in missed opportunities. But capital cannot exist without rules, without detailed laws regulating business transactions, without stable laws guaranteeing title to agreed returns. Without extensive public infrastructure a system of profit maximisation simply won't develop. Capital needs governments or rulers for the stable, predictable, but highly coercive enforcement of its unrestrained wishes.

Market propaganda always avoids the word *monopoly*, whilst making the most of *efficiency*, which aims to convince workers of their own expendability.

Globalisation. For maximum competition and profit, the system must take root as extensively as possible, but, at the same time, any similarly universal consequences that threaten capital must be combatted. That is why markets are not entirely well disposed to globalisation. Capital embraces nation states, whose varying and competitive tax laws offer useful niches to cache and save. Borders create markets with competitive prices for raw materials and labour.

Capital always has its suitcase packed, constantly threatening to leave countries unwilling or unable to satisfy its one-sided needs.

Property. Whereas the property-owning minority is obsessed with setting every advantageous legal aspect of ownership in stone, it doesn't want to extend these sweeping rights and privileges to the majority. A system of sustained appropriation will not tolerate growth of other people's property, and by extension liberty. Although markets seem to want to inundate us with new possessions, their survival requires our dispossession. We don't own the means of production and we're supposed to sell what we do own, our labour, immediately. Wholesale use of licensing, patents, and especially debt, allows capital to ultimately seize even the last of what we thought we'd earned. We'll never be allowed to call something our own for long, we'll have to keep working for others' private interests. Debt is a useful means of upholding this servility. It's another instance of the oppressive imbalance in power, the chasm between minority and majority rights: whereas the impossibility of *our* debts results in material loss, evictions, repossessions, and a strangled existence, the debts of the one per cent are the object of wily negotiation or profitable blackmail. The latest banking crisis has again shown that debts don't represent real value; shorn of their financial and political masks, they are no more than a lever of power.

Growth. It seems a fertile word, but capitalism isn't like a tree in need of constant connection to the earth to push its crown up to the heavens. Capital's compulsive pursuit of growth is driven by instability, the revolutionary energy that ruthlessly breaks open new sources of profit. One man's meat is another man's poison: no growth without its opposite. Industries gone to the wall, hereditary poverty, poisoned land: short-term gain on the one hand and draconian consequences for generations on the other. Non-economic factors like government regulation and charity assuage the system's worst effects, underwriting the crimes of capital.

Capital, with its oppressive property rights, cannot possibly exist without collective loss.

The overwrought accumulation of capital, overproduction, an uncontrollable mountain of waste, the daily threat of over-processed foods, a natural world increasingly changing from a bringer of sustenance to an avenger, governments transferring communal resources and power to the few through a process of deregulation and privatisation, unbridled inequality between the one per cent and our overwhelming majority — all these things endanger us. So many of us are so close to the edge.

Why do we so endlessly invest in our own disempowerment?

II

It's personal.

In the end, you see, capitalism is just another theory that works better on paper than in practice, a temporary idea we keep submitting to with false hopes and warranted fears. Just an idea — with real consequences and repercussions, and with real victims, it is true, but its sway is instantly jeopardised once an alternative catches on.

An incomparably prosperous, influential but vulnerable minority is trying to make us, the overwhelming majority, believe that our exploitation is natural and advantageous. Big bosses who, without any connection to a specific society or without proper accountability to any government institution or organisation, have successfully co-opted practically every state's authority. A minority with more money than power, more say than justified by its scant numbers. There are simply too few rich people. If the plutocracy were an army, then each of their gold-encrusted soldiers would come up against ninety-nine of us.

An intuitive understanding of humankind is essential to successful deceit. A conman can't afford to miss a trick; he has to incorporate and predict our actions, dreams and desires; he has to both despise and desire us. Having weaponised everything worthwhile in himself, he assesses other people's motives, mostly through the vulnerabilities they display. A conman understands that fear is a powerful tool to ensnare his prey and it is one of the hardest vulnerabilities to shake. He'll emphasise innate qualities useful to him, our supposedly inevitable resentment, selfishness, grievance and the like; he'll say what we want to hear, what he supposes we've been thinking all along. He'll institute penalties for good faith and reward suspicion. He's cynically amazed by his success, people's willingness to be his victims. The contempt this induces encourages him to feed our suspicions even more, using our imagination against us like parents punishing a disobedient child.

No faith without surrender, without believers craving to justify their submission and dress it up with proofs. Doubt is for the weak, alternatives are inconceivable, criticism can only come from criminals. The frauds have achieved their ultimate goal: our own willing self-deception.

A market economy can only succeed in a society, a culture in which social relations display the same market dynamics, with personal competition determining relationships, and the resulting divisions and struggles pushing some people to the wayside, where they have little choice but to sacrifice themselves for the social capital of an increasingly exclusive group. But being forced to operate under this unfavourable social contract, and suffering its oppressive, corrosive effects is not enough; we're then expected to accept our supposed destiny, even defend it.

Are humans competitive animals with an economic instinct? Did the reptiles we once were clamber onto a dry shore do so in order to take their first steps towards capitalism, meekly bowing their heads when they eventually discovered it? Why do people make an appeal to human nature when reality clashes with their inner self? Why do they only seem to use this mechanism when they can't reconcile the conflict with facts and reason?

To mask its fragile basis and temporary nature, capital must intervene in the human imagination. As with all dogma, facts have to be discredited, because facts give immediate reasons for resistance, irrefutable evidence of alternatives. With all its exploitation and deliberate reliance on fear and dependence, with data showing only a fraction of humanity benefits from the system, the reality of capitalism would be its own immediate and definitive deterrent. For capitalism to succeed it must, like religion, follow a path of mythology. If we don't want to believe our eyes, a story is what we need, one that's more convincing than credible.

It's 'human nature' and carefully selected items from the lucky dip of the past provide the evidence. The history of humankind becomes the story of its economic freedom, how it overcame more and more barriers over the centuries to express its 'natural' instinct for competition and free trade. Increasingly independent people succeeded in throwing off the yoke of the nobility and church, finally breaking free of stifling hierarchies and determining their own fate, finally able to keep everything for themselves.

The minority enriching itself at our expense desperately needs our help. As usual when crafting creation stories, its historians work backwards, creating a past for the intended present. Ideology doesn't come 'naturally' to humankind; an iron grip on our thoughts takes time and resources. The energy and expense needed to ensure our indoctrination are immense. We live under capitalism — everything that reaches us has first passed through its coercive filter. Every book, every film, all town planning, every note in our ears, every spoonful in our mouths, every brash newspaper headline, every movement and every word on every screen in front of us is a commodity that must produce a return, must create the conditions to secure ongoing profit. The central point is not that we must all interminably buy things, but that we are people who identify our needs as expressed perfectly by market needs, accepting the utility and necessity of our submission and exploitation.

Both economically and socially, capitalism is obviously a conscious construction. Historically, it has fed off the emancipatory achievements of the Enlightenment, things like secularisation, globalisation and egalitarianism, but it has finally emerged as a revaluation of hierarchy, segregating humanity in an imposed social order, a continuation of the minority's perpetual triumph over the majority. Traditional forces like the nobility and church end up siding with capital as capital maintains the status quo, and by inference the relationships that characterised an older, less enlightened world.

But we're still the overwhelming majority. Doesn't capital celebrate the power of numbers? The more the merrier; right is whatever turns out to be popular. Why do we seem unable to remove the barriers harming our interests?

No constitution gives us an enforceable right to a decent life. Instead now we feel the pressure of market-dominated governments that dismiss our needs as unnecessary, wasteful requests for handouts, or as risky, unsecured investments. This ideological unwillingness focuses on extending our deprivation, reducing our autonomy and increasing our fear.

Yet we're still the majority. We have power over the exploitative minority through the ballot box.

Why hasn't democracy yet solved this imbalance of power?

Gratification *before* need. Capital orders things so and in so doing weakens our resistance, undermines our defences, and makes us susceptible to hopeless conformism. A numbing, intoxicating order, its effects as crippling as they are predictable.

To become and remain market people, we must propagate the dynamics independently. We must independently subordinate our formative elements to market needs. What better way of stifling the freedom essential to satisfying ourselves than by putting instant gratification first? The brief sensation of satiety always disrupts the full range of human need, the necessity of deep and lasting fulfilment. The question of how to live runs up against appealing, greedy solutions through much smaller and more trivial issues.

Who can be bothered with questions about essential freedoms when an overwhelming supply atomises our concerns into endlessly satiable domains?

Gratification *before* need. How addictive it is to celebrate the wrong kind of agency, to feel like a liberated consumer of goods, services and information. Before we can see the outline of our future, we've let ourselves be seduced by the present; before we can really take in our present, we have set off in pursuit of countless fleeting delights. How toxic this delusion of control is, decision after decision after decision drawing us deeper into a hostile system.

Take the internet. So chaotic and gigantic that no one really seems responsible for it, a free zone with free admission for all our free desires. But freedom is nothing but a pipe dream in an environment dominated by profit maximisation and decimating competition, a domain characterised by a dearth of organised solidarity and democratic authority. Entangled with almost everything, this Moloch is the extraordinary triumph of the communications industry, of capital. Like at the dawn of capitalism, the system has used revolutionary developments to force the majority to bow to its indispensability. As well as our bread, capital has now appropriated our means of communication; all information and exchange are now subject to the profiting minority's approval. Nobody seems to own the internet until business interests are threatened. The internet seems to spring from nowhere, until taxes menace a source. Our privacy is a commodity; data about our lives, a free resource in the digital industry.

Now a global and seemingly elusive system that inextricably coerces societies, it has become an almost perfect regime. Every fresh click is another reinforcement of our captive dependence. With our real time and attention, and with a lot of real money, we invest in the continuation of our subjugation.

Gratification *before* need. Like other narcotics, this order poisons genuine desires for comfort, relief and connection with destructive doses of impossible dreams. Tempting little packets of fulfilment. Compartmentalisation and privatisation, two pillars of capitalism, have ensured their future.

We have come to look at ourselves differently, we have difficulty reaching our loved ones, we grope helplessly for explanations. Market needs have privatised us. We're afraid of losing ownership of ourselves if we aren't productive enough, if we don't manage to mix the personal with production, if we don't get one to profit from the other. Selling oneself as the ultimate self-fulfilment. A futile sacrifice; we are the ones who have exchanged our perspective for capital.

Even our identity, our consciousness of who we are, is unsafe. Capital realises that opposites can sap each other in conflict and lapse into conformity. Capital needs clear categories, classifiable and competitive labour units, and predictable markets. The freedom to set our own course, how and with whom we wish to organise our lives and the world around us, is too amorphous and mercurial — it doesn't pay well enough. Capital will always want to determine who we are.

Our identities are open ended. Every form of limitation is imposed by markets, they alone question who we are. No one can put a price tag on our identities, our inner selves can't be factored into a profit calculation.

That is why capital loves taboo. What else must constantly avail itself of euphemisms and other obscuring formulations to force reality to do its bidding, conceal its dangers and secrets, engineer coercive arrangements for production and labour, cast a shadow over freedom and individuality, and glorify conformism and obedience? Who benefits most from censorship? The vulnerable, powerful minority, or the overwhelming majority, which has the world to win by breaking capitalist taboos?

All coercion and indoctrination to stop resistance from developing are signs of a fundamental insecurity. There's something to hide. Clearly our initiatives, our free and creative capacity to shape our own lives, must be matched by organised distrust and consciously curbed. There can be no doubt that capital has misgivings about the outcome of the power struggle between its minority and our majority.

The secret's out. Capital is scared of us.

III

Whoever looks for support, a way of voicing suspicions of inequality and injustice; whoever is compelled or obliged by their growing awareness to take a critical view of our society — the environment that produced and continues to influence us; whoever searches for facts about previous generations and encounters only the versions and opinions of a limited class of interested parties, fiction delivered as history, stories with a one-sided presentation of main characters and heroes; whoever starts distrusting their own background and upbringing, gradually noticing correlations and the consequences of misleading information; whoever grasps that our limited time on earth demands something more meaningful than ceaseless buying and selling; whoever seeks help because their way of life and immediate future are under threat, seeing fear reflected every day in the faces of colleagues, friends and family; whoever is stimulated by this fear to think and act; whoever, after discovering that society deliberately creates powerless people, strives for their emancipation in the conviction that nobody is free until everyone is; whoever is themselves one of the powerless whose oppression stifles them but whose courage and hope drive them to act according to their freely chosen goals; whoever has been woken from befuddled denial by trauma, windfall or some other upending experience to find a beleaguered world of private gain and collective loss, with a damaged and wrathful environment, and is prepared to fight, a fight that is signalled by a newfound solidarity with the majority; whoever rejects being separated from the collective security of the majority for the destructive gains of the minority; whoever resists; whoever shows themselves; whoever wants to liberate themselves, champion other people and recognise the legal and moral equality of all will sooner or later come into contact with communism and feel welcomed.

In the most general sense, 'communism' means the collective pursuit of an egalitarian society in which knowledge, power, and income are fairly distributed. A society whose future lies in communally formulated rights and communally formulated duties, in other words a society that functions under rigorous democratic authority.

Communism insists on the abolition of hierarchy, of unfairly imposed imbalances in power. Instead of the exploitative machinations of capital, of a selfish elite, communism offers a free interplay of needs and talents, relying on the majority with all its unexpected and creative possibilities. Instead of the neurotic accumulation and extravagance of the minority, communism offers collective recognition of utility and the communal distribution of costs. Instead of property rights that favour the minority and expropriate the rest, communism offers the real value of property, personal goods that bear fruit without enslaving others or making them subordinate to those goods or that production. Instead of legally, economically and socially arbitrary borders and nation states, communism offers the shared destiny of all people on earth. Instead of incessant privatisation, communism offers solidarity that guarantees individual autonomy. Instead of the inevitable selfishness of profit, communism offers inalienable rights to common property, to basic necessities. Instead of the omnipotence of one particular and very limited caste, communism offers the classless redemption of democracy. As an idea, it offers a potentially truly equitable system of representation and accountability.

IV

But communism is a concept with a turbulent history. An idea about people and society that hasn't had an easy path. A word that is inseparable from the influences that have determined its reputation and tradition. Over the past two centuries, communism has been applied and invoked in many different forms.

Hellish dictatorships have used communist rhetoric and communist concepts for repressive and lethal ends. For children of the Cold War, communism is the name of an old nemesis that proved contrived and unsustainable in the face of our inevitable future. The communist states we know left high death tolls in their wake. Stalin, Mao, Castro, Pol Pot: names that fill us with horror. For the masses trampled underfoot by these despots, communism was justification for oppression, a rigid euphemism whose invocation always spelt disaster. A dogma that had a clear view of its foes and was ready to immediately punish all who formed a threat. Penal colonies, purges, secret services hounding forbidden thoughts. The affected generations have no doubts about communism's abject culpability.

1848. 'A spectre is haunting Europe — the spectre of Communism.' The opening line of *The Communist Manifesto* written by Marx and Engels. This spectre wasn't a frightening figure to the victims of the nineteenth century, the men, women and children in factories and mines, the men, women and children on colonial plantations. Capitalism had entrenched itself all over the world. With the aid of governments, aggressive profiteers drove their industrial and colonial empires deeper into societies. With their profits, this new, more prescient nobility oversaw the impoverishment of current and future workers, ordered the expulsion or enslavement of indigenous peoples in potentially resource-rich areas, bought mansions and luxurious garments, carriages and country residences, immortalised themselves in paint or bronze, maintained close political contacts.

Democratic authority couldn't control these profiteers; it would be some time before *all* voices were included in communal decisions about justice and injustice. Slavery still existed; wars of conquest drew new borders. America's young democracy had the same contradictions as its ancient Greek predecessor: a society built on the backs of slaves, with voting rights reserved for free, 'ethnically pure' men.

In Europe, too, nineteenth-century men, women and children were, like us, free to enter into contracts; there were no armed guards at the factory gates to stop workers fleeing. But anyone who didn't work put everything on the line. Even those who worked were exposed and alone. Only charity occasionally lent succour, support that was often conditional thanks to the far-reaching influence of religion and the morality of the day. Illness could be a death sentence, families were shattered, poverty was hereditary, and when industrialists moved on to new seams of profit, the areas they left behind slid into irrevocable destitution.

Communists like Marx and Engels investigated and interpreted this exploitation of people by people, placed it in a historical perspective, and criticised it. In their pamphlet, they call for resistance, for revolution, for the overthrow of the ruling classes: 'In short, the Communists everywhere support every revolutionary movement against the existing social and political order of things. [...] They labour everywhere for the union and agreement of the democratic parties of all countries.' Communism has many thinkers and perspectives, numerous schools and positions, and entrenched divisions, but each version focused on the emancipation of the oppressed majority.

Under capitalism, all suppression is exploitation. Communism provided a language and insights for emancipation; it was up to future collectives to develop them. What are capital's traps and disruptive methods; how can they be avoided; what does revolution mean; which of a community's problems must be alleviated first; how do you unite different people in the same position; how can solidarity help resolve class struggle? Never before in history had the majority invoked its power in this way. Communists formulated ideas and ideals, questions as to how to carry on living together arose from visions of an as yet unknown world.

Armed with collective needs and desires, newly formed workers' movements tried to improve their members' lives. For the first time, the working majority, united in trade unions, stood up for its own well-being and future. The power of numbers, of solidarity, with organised groups whose representatives stuck to their mission, balancing conflicting interests. This emergent communism was in effect trying to invent a working democracy.

Societies developed, each from its own history and in its own way. Power refuses to be redistributed when it has been concentrated in the same restricted places for too long.
The profiteers were able to carry on as before. The one per cent maintained its grip on the means of production and unquestioned

access to the corridors of power. Despite predictably fierce opposition, communists continued to doggedly assail the unjust order.

One of the most notable thinkers *and* activists to expand Marx's theory of class struggle and criticism of the political economy was Rosa Luxemburg. Born in 1871 in Russian-controlled Poland, close to the Russian border, in an intellectual and cosmopolitan milieu, she was an exceptional and gifted child. Although she suffered physical ailments from a young age and walked with a limp, her boundless energy and intellectual curiosity were more important in shaping her life. She drew and painted, read Polish, German, Russian and French literature, wrote poetry in all those languages, and cultivated a life-long interest in history, anthropology, botany and geology. Her iconoclasm and sense of justice were equally precocious: as a sixteen-year-old secondary-school pupil in Warsaw she helped organise national strikes. Three years later her political activities had forced her to flee to Switzerland, where she earned a doctorate in both philosophy and law at the University of Zurich. Luxemburg joined several socialist and communist organisations and parties, developed Marx's doctrines, wrote and organised, gave speeches and travelled. She noted these thoughts in 1918: 'far from being a sum of ready-made prescriptions which have only to be applied, the practical realisation of socialism as an economic, social and juridical system is something which lies completely hidden in the mists of the future. What we possess in our programme is nothing but a few main signposts which indicate the general direction in which to look for the necessary measures, and the indications are mainly negative in character at that. [...]
The negative, the tearing down, can be decreed; the building up, the positive, cannot. New Territory. A thousand problems. Only experience is capable of correcting and opening new ways. Only unobstructed, effervescing life falls into a thousand new forms and improvisations, brings to light creative new force, itself corrects all mistaken attempts.'

Social progress was too slow, certainly from the victims' perspective, but the trial of strength between capital and the majority delivered some initial successes. What had previously been impossible seemed to become reality. In some European countries the incidental nature of charity started being supplanted by enforceable regulatory and legal structures. Living conditions gradually improved, and confidence in the realism and legitimacy of democratic authority grew. The majority dared to claim a central place in the future. All contemporary achievements related to autonomy and solidarity, from limits on the working week to labour protection, from education to health care and popular representation in government, are grounded in communist intentions and principles.

1917. The first major socialist-inspired revolution in the world broke out in Russia. Centuries-old tsarist rule had been weakened by the First World War, and runaway inflation and a pressing shortage of all basic needs sparked massive strikes. A chain reaction of demonstrations, strikes and armed resistance was ignited in early 1917. Popular support for the revolution increased when Tsar Nicolas II dissolved the Duma. The unexpectedly far-reaching uprising surprised everyone; more than a thousand people died in the turmoil. Soldiers revolted, refusing to shoot demonstrators. The February Revolution forced the tsar's abdication. Whilst most socialist leaders were either languishing in Siberia or exiled abroad, a motley coalition of revolutionaries established a Provisional Government. The new freedoms and rights introduced by the Provisional Government contrasted sharply with the absolutism of the tsarist era. As well as freedom of expression, press and assembly, it introduced universal suffrage for women and men. Laws upholding religious, ethnic or class discrimination were repealed. Tsarist imperialism was relegated to the past. The death penalty was also abolished.

Rosa Luxemburg wrote: 'Freedom only for the supporters of the government, only for the members of one party — however numerous they may be — is no freedom at all. Freedom is always and exclusively freedom for the one who thinks differently. Not because of any fanatical concept of "justice" but because all that is instructive, wholesome and purifying in political freedom depends on this essential characteristic, and its effectiveness vanishes when "freedom" becomes a special privilege.'

The 1917 revolution took a new turn in April, when Lenin returned from years of exile. His idea for a new order reeked of the old regime. Instead of promoting justice and democracy, Lenin and his Bolsheviks fed discontent. He stirred up nationalist sentiment, encouraged violence, retribution and reckless expropriation. The Bolshevik's October Revolution — his brainchild — was nothing more than a power grab, a bid for dictatorship.

This came as no surprise to Rosa Luxemburg, who had noted as early as 1904 that 'the ultra-centralism asked by Lenin is full of the sterile spirit of the overseer. It is not a positive and creative spirit. *Lenin's concern is not so much to make the activity of the party more fruitful as to control the party — to narrow the movement rather than to develop it, to bind rather than to unify it.*' Luxemburg had foreseen how Lenin's power-hungry interpretation of Marx would lead to a new dictatorship of a minority.

In 1919, Rosa Luxemburg was one of the leaders of the German Communist Party. After a poorly prepared, unpopular and abortive revolution, which she had led against her better judgement, she was arrested, tortured and executed without trial. Months later, her body was found floating in a lock on Berlin's Landwehr Canal.

The Soviet Union was founded in 1922. The victory of Lenin's tyrannical Central Committee was to determine the future of communism in the twentieth century. Lenin had developed the blueprint for every totalitarian regime intent on luring genuinely suffering peoples with false communist promises.

Capital needed the right enemy and disguise. The Cold War provided an almost perfect context for both. With the Soviets' manifestly repressive and unfree state power as the alternative, the United States had no difficulty justifying its own brand of capitalism — with all its exploitation and pollution, with all its social exclusion and rapacious imperialism — as the free and inevitable standard for all societies. Latterly the centrally planned economies of the Soviet Union and China provided useful cover for the unbridled economic monopolies of the American political elite. In none of the totalitarian, supposedly communist states did the majority own the means of production; in no way and at no time were their populations ever masters of their own destiny. Stalin developed ruthless state capitalism to benefit his regime. Russia was a gargantuan enterprise, with a cheap, downtrodden workforce, flexibly priced raw materials, a guaranteed market, sham production and turnover figures, and perennially exultant and supine media. Large contemporary enterprises would relish comparable levels of capitalist control.

East versus West: a binary contest with artificial, politically profitable contrasts. The extreme of Soviet communism provided Americans with a foil for every criticism of capitalism. The cobbled together Soviet Union experienced the height of its unity; communists around the world clung to its exaggerated success, beleaguered and persecuted in their capitalist homelands. Longing for a life-fulfilling justification, they patiently bided time for a comparable revolution to become a sacred mission. The Red Tsar got off scot-free.

Why didn't the western powers design to learn from the emancipation of the former Eastern Bloc after the fall of the Berlin Wall? Countries and peoples whose future was, at that time, guided only by freedom, not weighed down by the West's fixed and restrictive economic idiom, and without the oppressive inequality it causes: did Europe assimilate these countries too quickly?

Why the insecurity? Why did democracy and capitalism have to be conflated? Why promise wealth which by historical standards was impossible to achieve?

Europe welcomed its liberated region as one might a conquered territory. Who is now surprised therefore by reactive fascist and antidemocratic sympathies in the former Eastern Bloc?

Developing new democracies, the rule of law, new foundations for fairer self-determination; a nascent majority keen to shape a just collective future based on the common good, together creating the conditions for durable freedom, a humane economy and environmental recovery: who wouldn't want to play a constructive role in that? The moment passed. Europe missed a precious opportunity.

And communism? Surely we've seen that it doesn't work, that it only leads to atrocities? Perpetrated by dictatorial elites, but laid at the door of unimplemented ideals: who can ever clear up such a misunderstanding?

*

Every ideology ends in the torture chamber: it's curious how seldom the theory of the degeneration of ideologies is applied to capitalism.

*

Who profits from the denial and disappearance of communism?

V

Life is a process of learning how to live. It means continually adapting to circumstances, other people's actions, unexpected movements and change.

Increasing autonomy and reducing fear.

Distress narrows consciousness, fear slows us down and casts shadows over the future. We're obsessed by longings — we can't help it — we see them clearly in our imagination and disappear into personal worlds to taste of our dreams, to safely trial our hopes. We are each unique — that's simply so. Where and how we come into the world, always in slightly different places, slightly different ways, determines the course of our lives. Experiences shape us, creating boundaries but also possibilities, the lifelong cycle of achievement and loss.

Our imagination isn't completely free; it seems paradoxical that our deepest motivator is tied to so many forces outside ourselves. We are partly our influences. Yet the actions resulting from those influences are also uniquely our own. Our nature can be pieced together from our actions; how we express ourselves reveals our desires. It's an individual process, an inextricable part of who we are.

But our *collective* desires deserve the same scope for fulfilment as our individual needs. Collective desires are the foundations on which we can build our personal dreams.

The freedom of our imagination has always been a political issue, our imagination is too headstrong for our rulers to trust, they have always wanted to manipulate it for their own gain. Their mistrust was well founded — if they hadn't been able to influence us so deeply, we would never have accepted and helped maintain their illegitimate power. Our imagination is a weapon which must be brought to heel. This makes our very existence deeply political.

Opposition to a system that endangers our individual needs is rooted in our imagination, which is also the source of its power. We need to protect, nurture and strengthen that imagination, and doing so is a political act, realising the political power in every one of us. The time has come to act according to that power.

We're entitled to be in charge of our decisions, to reclaim our imaginations as valued possessions. It's up to our collective desires to safeguard this possession.

*

We must eat to stay alive. Food producers haven't had any trouble asserting their rights. Yet we have no right to food. Their entitlement to withhold our food is greater than our claim to an essential element of our existence. Even when producing our own food, slaughtering or harvesting it, they can forbid us from eating it. The right to let someone else go hungry is enshrined in more laws than our natural need for food. Who benefits from this?

Without a roof over our heads each of us plunges into free fall, but we have lost a right to housing. Through contractors and developers and slumlords and banks, again these rights have been accrued by these powers.

And healthcare. Whilst some post-war governments established national healthcare systems, the pharmaceutical industry has been left to its own devices. This omission costs societies crushing amounts of public funds. Life-saving pills or treatments are another common good we can't lay claim to. Doctors have their oath, but it's the insurers who really call the shots when it comes to our health.

The technological infrastructure through which we keep in touch and provide each other with information has become indispensable to human communication in the modern world. But how much power do we have over an arena determined by markets? The internet isn't supposed to belong to anyone, but it certainly isn't ours. We contribute to this domain every day without being granted a say in it. How can something so universal and influential be outside our communal control?

A right to life isn't worth anything if the earth can no longer sustain us, if its climate and fertility turn away from us. Our greatest shared good is the most essential.

*

The final authority over human need is now the market. This makes governments permanently susceptible to blackmail and harms society. Our economies are conscious constructions; if capital took human form, it would howl with laughter at the cynicism with which we pay for our own submission and exploitation.

Communal goods, the shared conditions for our existence, increase our autonomy and reduce our fear. Communal goods are the expression of our collective desires.

We're not pursuing the kind of expropriation capitalism has inflicted on us for centuries. We're not an unjustly dominant minority. Communal goods must be carefully looked after, which is why the shared needs for our existence must be under democratic control, so we might use a system of representation and accountability to jointly determine the design of their direction.

Democratic authority offers the opportunity to distribute power fairly. Once we have responsibly and representatively secured our communal goods, power can spread equitably through the majority. Only under such conditions will a basic universal income be able to deliver the promise of a liberated existence.

'From each according to their abilities, to each according to their needs': every freedom and opportunity is encapsulated in this desire. The future is uncertain, but we must enjoy it in freedom. Even now communism is trying to devise a true working democracy.

A word about love.

For now, we're living in the past. Old myths, stubborn systems and inflexible interests constrict our ideas about wealth and poverty, power and impotence. This gives the present little opportunity to develop independently, little space to renew itself in each generation for an unconstrained future.

How long has the minority been dictating our bondage?

Not much can be done about death, of course, but all our lives, experiences and memories crave meaning. How can we do justice to the breadth of our existence? When will we finally be entitled to express our true selves safely?

Grounding a future in the present demands courage, fearlessness to trust in a tomorrow that can't be foreseen by looking to the past.

Communism opposes capital to try to bring about a fairer world, but Rosa Luxemburg was right when she wrote, 'the negative, the tearing down, can be decreed; the building up, the positive, *cannot*.'

What should an egalitarian society be like? What might happen as hierarchies disappear? What will our lives be like as the role of work changes? What responsibilities come with the political agency we will attain? What response will our resistance provoke? Many of these things are unknowable, questions that will remain open until new experiences provide answers.

It's all right to have doubts, to hesitate, or stray. Our lives consist of endless attempts and continual adjustments. Although the hopes that drive us should be proclaimed, mistakes and misunderstandings will always dog us. But each confrontation between desire and reality can produce useful alternatives. Each inevitable failure is followed by endless improvement.

*

When we speak of faith, of the hope that must withstand the unexpected, we mean that love will have to lend us a hand. There's nothing strange about a more universal and profound association between people being produced by the driving force of love. But lovelessness breeds self-hatred, a crippling privatisation. It's in doing something for others that we start existing for ourselves.

*

Collective desire comes with the liberating realisation that we're not alone. A future in which we no longer allow ourselves to be atomised awaits.

*

Once we affirm each other's courage and freedom, the right to exploit others will be finished.

*

Let's agree to call it a revolution once we have freed ourselves from capital and are finally able to turn to the true question: how do we live collectively free?

It's not too late. It is not too late.

Sisters, brothers, it's up to us.

nieuw new
dutch **nederlands**
stemmen voices

VERZET is a series of chapbooks showcasing the work of some of the most exciting writers working in Dutch today, published by Strangers Press, part of the UEA Publishing Project.

Each story is beautifully translated and presented as an individual chapbook, with a design inspired by the text in collaboration with The Dutch Foundation for Literature and National Centre for Writing.

1 **RECONSTRUCTION**
   by Karin Amatmoekrim trans. by Sarah Timmer Harvey

2 **THANK YOU FOR BEING WITH US**
   by Thomas Heerma van Voss, trans. by Moshe Gilula

3 **BERGJE**
   by Bregje Hofstede trans. by Alice Tetley-Paul

4 **THE TOURIST BUTCHER**
   by Jamal Ouariachi trans. by Scott Emblen-Jarrett

5 **RESIST! IN DEFENCE OF COMMUNISM**
   by Gustaaf Peek trans. by Brendan Monaghan

6 **THE DANDY**
   by Nina Polak trans. by Emma Rault

7 **SHELTER**
   by Sanneke van Hassel trans. by Danny Guinan

8 **SOMETHING HAS TO HAPPEN**
   by Maartje Wortle trans. by Jozef van der Voort

Supported by
N National Centre for Writing
N ederlands letterenfonds dutch foundation for literature

This series was made possible by generous funding from The Dutch Foundation for Literature